Praise for
The Trouble with Poetry

"Collins's accessible and deeply human poetry would make a poetry lover out of anyone." —*Good Housekeeping*

"[This] new collection by Collins . . . should bolster his standing as America's most popular poet. All the poems in *The Trouble with Poetry* are accessible and thoughtful, many are funny, and worth reading aloud. . . . [His poems contain] a kind of frank optimism or benevolence that is . . . simply warm and human." —*Virginia Quarterly*

"Collins is as close as anyone in contemporary American poetry will likely get to being a household name. Blame his sweet, smart, and wise poems . . . his colorful personality and ungoverned humor; or his remarkable energy. . . . This collection is as rich and mischievous as anything he has given us previously. Highly recommended." —*Library Journal*

"Disarming . . . and devastatingly funny . . . Skeptical of love and scornful of pretension, Collins is breathtaking in his appreciation of the earth's beauty and the precious daily routines that define life." —*Booklist*

"Collins has a firm grasp of his art and craft. . . . If he gives a reading near you, by all means go. You might just get hooked on poetry." —*The Washington Times*

"Charming . . . With his wit and plainspokenness, Collins is a likeable successor to Robert Frost." —Cleveland *Plain Dealer*

Also by Billy Collins

THE TROUBLE WITH
POETRY

THE TROUBLE WITH
POETRY

And Other Poems

BILLY COLLINS

RANDOM HOUSE TRADE PAPERBACKS

New York

2007 Random House Trade Paperback Edition

Copyright © 2005 by Billy Collins

Published in the United States by Random House Trade
Paperbacks, an imprint of The Random House Publishing Group,
a division of Random House, Inc., New York.

RANDOM HOUSE TRADE PAPERBACKS and colophon are
trademarks of Random House, Inc.

Originally published in hardcover in the United States
by Random House, an imprint of The Random House
Publishing Group, a division of Random House, Inc., in 2005.

Previous publication information about some of the poems
contained within this work can be found beginning on page 87.

ISBN 978-0-375-75521-7

Library of Congress Cataloging-in-Publication Data

Collins, Billy.
The trouble with poetry: and other poems / Billy Collins.
p.   cm.
ISBN 978-0-375-75521-7
I. Title: Trouble with poetry.   II. Title.
PS3553.O47478T76 2005
811'.54—dc22   2005046562

Printed in the United States of America

6 8 9 7 5

Book design by Dana Leigh Blanchette

To my students and my teachers

My idea of paradise is a perfect automobile
going thirty miles an hour on a smooth road
to a twelfth-century cathedral.

—HENRY JAMES

Contents

THE TROUBLE WITH
POETRY

You, Reader

I wonder how you are going to feel
when you find out
that I wrote this instead of you,

that it was I who got up early
to sit in the kitchen
and mention with a pen

the rain-soaked windows,
the ivy wallpaper,
and the goldfish circling in its bowl.

Go ahead and turn aside,
bite your lip and tear out the page,
but, listen—it was just a matter of time

before one of us happened
to notice the unlit candles
and the clock humming on the wall.

Plus, nothing happened that morning—
a song on the radio,
a car whistling along the road outside—

and I was only thinking
about the shakers of salt and pepper
that were standing side by side on a place mat.

I wondered if they had become friends
after all these years
or if they were still strangers to one another

like you and I
who manage to be known and unknown
to each other at the same time—

me at this table with a bowl of pears,
you leaning in a doorway somewhere
near some blue hydrangeas, reading this.

ONE

Monday

The birds are in their trees,
the toast is in the toaster,
and the poets are at their windows.

They are at their windows
in every section of the tangerine of earth—
the Chinese poets looking up at the moon,
the American poets gazing out
at the pink and blue ribbons of sunrise.

The clerks are at their desks,
the miners are down in their mines,
and the poets are looking out their windows
maybe with a cigarette, a cup of tea,
and maybe a flannel shirt or bathrobe is involved.

The proofreaders are playing the ping-pong
game of proofreading,
glancing back and forth from page to page,
the chefs are dicing celery and potatoes,
and the poets are at their windows
because it is their job for which
they are paid nothing every Friday afternoon.

Which window it hardly seems to matter
though many have a favorite,

for there is always something to see—
a bird grasping a thin branch,
the headlights of a taxi rounding a corner,
those two boys in wool caps angling across the street.

The fishermen bob in their boats,
the linemen climb their round poles,
the barbers wait by their mirrors and chairs,
and the poets continue to stare
at the cracked birdbath or a limb knocked down by the wind.

By now, it should go without saying
that what the oven is to the baker
and the berry-stained blouse to the dry cleaner,
so the window is to the poet.

Just think—
before the invention of the window,
the poets would have had to put on a jacket
and a winter hat to go outside
or remain indoors with only a wall to stare at.

And when I say a wall,
I do not mean a wall with striped wallpaper
and a sketch of a cow in a frame.

I mean a cold wall of fieldstones,
the wall of the medieval sonnet,
the original woman's heart of stone,
the stone caught in the throat of her poet-lover.

Statues in the Park

I thought of you today
when I stopped before an equestrian statue
in the middle of a public square,

you who had once instructed me
in the code of these noble poses.

A horse rearing up with two legs raised,
you told me, meant the rider had died in battle.

If only one leg was lifted,
the man had elsewhere succumbed to his wounds;

and if four legs were touching the ground,
as they were in this case—
bronze hooves affixed to a stone base—
it meant that the man on the horse,

this one staring intently
over the closed movie theater across the street,
had died of a cause other than war.

In the shadow of the statue,
I wondered about the others
who had simply walked through life
without a horse, a saddle, or a sword—

pedestrians who could no longer
place one foot in front of the other.

I pictured statues of the sickly
recumbent on their cold stone beds,
the suicides toeing the marble edge,

statues of accident victims covering their eyes,
the murdered covering their wounds,
the drowned silently treading the air.

And there was I,
up on a rosy-gray block of granite
near a cluster of shade trees in the local park,
my name and dates pressed into a plaque,

down on my knees, eyes lifted,
praying to the passing clouds,
forever begging for just one more day.

Traveling Alone

At the hotel coffee shop that morning,
the waitress was wearing a pink uniform
with "Florence" written in script over her heart.

And the man who checked my bag
had a nameplate that said "Ben."
Behind him was a long row of royal palms.

On the plane, two women poured drinks
from a cart they rolled down the narrow aisle—
"Debbie" and "Lynn" according to their winged tags.

And such was my company
as I arced from coast to coast,
and so I seldom spoke, and then only

of the coffee, the bag, the tiny bottles of vodka.
I said little more than "Thank you"
and "Can you take this from me, please?"

Yet I began to sense that all of them
were ready to open up,
to get to know me better, perhaps begin a friendship.

Florence looked irritated
as she shuffled from table to table,
but was she just hiding her need

to know about my early years—
the ball I would toss and catch in my hands,
the times I hid behind my mother's dress?

And was I so wrong in seeing in Ben's eyes
a glimmer of interest in my theories
and habits—my view of the Enlightenment,

my love of cards, the hours I tended to keep?
And what about Debbie and Lynn?
Did they not look eager to ask about my writing process,

my way of composing in the morning
by a window, which I would have admitted
if they had just had the courage to ask.

And strangely enough—I would have continued
as they stopped pouring drinks
and the other passengers turned to listen—

the only emotion I ever feel, Debbie and Lynn,
is what the beaver must feel,
as he bears each stick to his hidden construction,

which creates the tranquil pond
and gives the mallards somewhere to paddle,
the pair of swans a place to conceal their young.

House

I lie in a bedroom of a house
that was built in 1862, we were told—
the two windows still facing east
into the bright daily reveille of the sun.

The early birds are chirping,
and I think of those who have slept here before,
the family we bought the house from—
the five Critchlows—

and the engineer they told us about
who lived here alone before them,
the one who built onto the back
of the house a large glassy room with wood beams.

I have an old photograph of the house
in black and white, a few small trees,
and a curved dirt driveway,
but I do not know who lived here then.

So I go back to the Civil War
and to the farmer who built the house
and the rough stone walls
that encompass the house and run up into the woods,

he who mounted his thin wife in this room,
while the war raged to the south,

with the strength of a dairyman
or with the tenderness of a dairyman

or with both, alternating back and forth
so as to give his wife much pleasure
and to call down a son to earth
to take over the cows and the farm

when he no longer had the strength
after all the days and nights of toil and prayer—
the sun breaking over the same horizon
into these same windows,

lighting the same bed-space where I lie
having nothing to farm, and no son,
the dead farmer and his dead wife for company,
feeling better and worse by turns.

In the Moment

It was a day in June, all lawn and sky,
the kind that gives you no choice
but to unbutton your shirt
and sit outside in a rough wooden chair.

And if a glass of ice tea and a volume
of seventeenth-century poetry
with a dark blue cover are available,
then the picture can hardly be improved.

I remember a fly kept landing on my wrist,
and two black butterflies
with white and red wing-dots
bobbed around my head in the bright air.

I could feel the day offering itself to me,
and I wanted nothing more
than to be in the moment—but which moment?
Not that one, or that one, or that one,

or any of those that were scuttling by
seemed perfectly right for me.
Plus, I was too knotted up with questions
about the past and his tall, evasive sister, the future.

What churchyard held the bones of George Herbert?
Why did John Donne's wife die so young?

And more pressingly,
what could we serve the vegetarian twins

who were coming to dinner that evening?
Who knew that they would bring their own grapes?
And why was the driver of that pickup
flying down the road toward the lone railroad track?

And so the priceless moments of the day
were squandered one by one—
or more likely a thousand at a time—
with quandary and pointless interrogation.

All I wanted was to be a pea of being
inside the green pod of time,
but that was not going to happen today,
I had to admit to myself

as I closed the book on the face
of Thomas Traherne and returned to the house
where I lit a flame under a pot
full of floating brown eggs,

and, while they cooked in their bubbles,
I stared into a small oval mirror near the sink
to see if that crazy glass
had anything special to tell me today.

The Peasants' Revolt

Soon enough it will all be over—
the shirt hanging from the doorknob,
trees beyond the windows,
and the kettle of water bubbling on a burner.

Soon enough, soon enough,
the many will be overwhelmed by the one.

Instead of the shaded road to the house,
the blue wheelbarrow upended,
and a picture book across my hips in bed,

just an expanse of white ink,
or a dark tunnel coiling away and down.

No sunflowers, no notebook,
no sand-colored denim jacket
and a piece of straw in the teeth,

just a hole inside a larger hole
and the starless maw of space.

But we are still here,
with all the world before us,
a beaded glass of water on the night table,
and the rest of this summer afternoon ahead.

So undo the buttons on your white blouse
and toss it over a chair back.
Let us lie down side by side
on these crisp sheets like two effigies on a tomb,
supine in a shadowy corner of a cathedral.

Let us be as still and serene
as Richard II and Anne of Bohemia—
he who ended the Peasants' Revolt so ruthlessly
and she to whom he was so devoted,
now entombed together, hand in stone hand.

Let us close our eyes to the white room
and let the fan blades on the ceiling cool us
as they turn like the hands of a speeding clock.

Theme

It's a sunny weekday in early May
and after a ham sandwich
and a cold bottle of beer on the brick terrace,

I am consumed by the wish
to add something
to one of the ancient themes—

youth dancing with his eyes closed,
for example,
in the shadows of corruption and death,

or the rise and fall of illustrious men
strapped to the turning
wheel of mischance and disaster.

There is a slight breeze,
just enough to bend
the yellow tulips on their stems,

but that hardly helps me
echo the longing for immortality
despite the roaring juggernaut of time,

or the painful motif
of Nature's cyclical return
versus man's blind rush to the grave.

I could loosen my shirt
and lie down in the soft grass,
sweet now after its first cutting,

but that would not produce
a record of the pursuit
of the moth of eternal beauty

or the despondency that attends
the eventual dribble
of the once gurgling fountain of creativity.

So, as far as the great topics go,
that seems to leave only
the fall from exuberant maturity

into sudden, headlong decline—
a subject that fills me with silence
and leaves me with no choice

but to spend the rest of the day
sniffing the jasmine vine
and surrendering to the ivory governance

of the piano by picking out
with my index finger
the melody notes of "Easy to Love,"

a song in which Cole Porter expresses,
with put-on nonchalance,
the hopelessness of a love

brimming with desire
and a hunger for affection,
but met only and always with frosty disregard.

Eastern Standard Time

Poetry speaks to all people, it is said,
but here I would like to address
only those in my own time zone,
this proper slice of longitude
that runs from pole to snowy pole
down the globe through Montreal to Bogotá.

Oh, fellow inhabitants of this singular band,
sitting up in your many beds this morning—
the sun falling through the windows
and casting a shadow on the sundial—
consider those in other zones who cannot hear these words.

They are not slipping into a bathrobe as we are,
or following the smell of coffee in a timely fashion.

Rather, they are at work already,
leaning on copy machines,
hammering nails into a house-frame.

They are not swallowing a vitamin like us;
rather they are smoking a cigarette under a half moon,
even jumping around on a dance floor,
or just now sliding under the covers,
pulling down the little chains on their bed lamps.

But we are not like these others,
for at this very moment on the face of the earth,
we are standing under a hot shower,

or we are eating our breakfast,
considered by people of all zones
to be the most important meal of the day.

Later, when the time is right,
we might sit down with the boss,
wash the car, or linger at a candle-lit table,
but now is the hour for pouring the juice
and flipping the eggs with one eye on the toaster.

So let us slice a banana and uncap the jam,
lift our brimming spoons of milk,
and leave it to the others to lower a flag
or spin absurdly in a barber's chair—
those antipodal oddballs, always early or late.

Let us praise Sir Stanford Fleming,
the Canadian genius who first scored
with these lines the length of the spinning earth.

Let us move together through the rest of this day
passing in unison from light to shadow,

coasting over the crest of noon
into the valley of the evening
and then, holding hands, slip into the deeper valley of night.

The Long Day

In the morning I ate a banana
like a young ape
and worked on a poem called "Nocturne."

In the afternoon I opened the mail
with a short kitchen knife,
and when dusk began to fall

I took off my clothes,
put on "Sweetheart of the Rodeo"
and soaked in a claw-footed bathtub.

I closed my eyes and thought
about the alphabet,
the letters filing out of the halls of kindergarten

to become literature.
If the British call *z* zed,
I wondered, why not call *b* bed and *d* dead?

And why does *z*, which looks like
the fastest letter, come at the very end?
unless they are all moving east

when we are facing north in our chairs.
It was then that I heard
a clap of thunder and the dog's bark,

and the claw-footed bathtub
took one step forward,
or was it backward

I had to ask
as I turned
to reach for a faraway towel.

TWO

I Ask You

What scene would I rather be enveloped in
than this one,
an ordinary night at the kitchen table,
at ease in a box of floral wallpaper,
white cabinets full of glass,
the telephone silent,
a pen tilted back in my hand?

It gives me time to think
about the leaves gathering in corners,
lichen greening the high gray rocks,
and the world sailing on beyond the dunes—
huge, oceangoing, history bubbling in its wake.

Outside of this room
there is nothing that I need,
not a job that would allow me to row to work,
or a coffee-colored Aston Martin DB4
with cracked green leather seats.

No, it is all right here,
the clear ovals of a glass of water,
a small crate of oranges, a book on Stalin,
an odd snarling fish in a frame on the wall,
and these three candles,
each a different height, singing in perfect harmony.

So forgive me
if I lower my head and listen
to the short bass candle as he takes a solo
while my heart
thrums under my shirt—
frog at the edge of a pond—
and my thoughts fly off to a province
composed of one enormous sky
and about a million empty branches.

Breathless

Some like the mountains, some like the seashore,
Jean-Paul Belmondo says
to the camera in the opening scene.

Some like to sleep face up,
some like to sleep on their stomachs,
I am thinking here in bed—

some take the shape of murder victims
flat on their backs all night,
others float face down on the dark waters.

Then there are those like me
who prefer to sleep on their sides,
knees brought up to the chest,

head resting on a crooked arm
and a soft fist touching the chin,
which is the way I would like to be buried,

curled up in a coffin
in a fresh pair of cotton pajamas,
a down pillow under my weighty head.

After a lifetime of watchfulness
and nervous vigilance,
I will be more than ready for sleep,

so never mind the dark suit,
the ridiculous tie
and the pale limp hands crossed on the chest.

Lower me down in my slumber,
tucked into myself
like the oldest fetus on earth,

and while cows look over the stone wall
of the cemetery, let me rest here
in my earthy little bedroom,

my lashes glazed with ice,
the roots of trees inching nearer,
and no dreams to frighten me anymore.

In the Evening

The heads of roses begin to droop.
The bee who has been hauling his gold
all day finds a hexagon in which to rest.

In the sky, traces of clouds,
the last few darting birds,
watercolors on the horizon.

The white cat sits facing a wall.
The horse in the field is asleep on its feet.

I light a candle on the wood table.
I take another sip of wine.
I pick up an onion and a knife.

And the past and the future?
Nothing but an only child with two different masks.

Bereft

I liked listening to you today at lunch
as you talked about the dead,
the lucky dead you called them,
citing their freedom from rent and furniture,

no need for doorknobs, snow shovels,
or windows and a field beyond,
no more railway ticket in an inside pocket,
no more railway, no more tickets, no more pockets.

No more bee chasing you around the garden,
no more you chasing your hat around a corner,
no bright moon on the glimmering water,
no cool breast felt beneath an open robe.

More like an empty zone that souls traverse,
a vaporous place
at the end of a dark tunnel,
a region of silence except for

the occasional beating of wings—
and, I wanted to add
as the sun dazzled your lifted wineglass,
the sound of the newcomers weeping.

Flock

It has been calculated that each copy of the
Gutenburg Bible . . . required the skins of 300 sheep.
—from an article on printing

I can see them squeezed into the holding pen
behind the stone building
where the printing press is housed,

all of them squirming around
to find a little room
and looking so much alike

it would be nearly impossible
to count them,
and there is no telling

which one will carry the news
that the Lord is a shepherd,
one of the few things they already know.

Boyhood

Alone in the basement,
I would sometimes lower one eye
to the level of the narrow train track

to watch the puffing locomotive
pull the cars around a curve
then bear down on me with its dazzling eye.

What was in those moments
before I lifted my head and let the train
go rocking by under my nose?

I remember not caring much
about the fake grass or the buildings
that made up the miniature town.

The same went for the station and its master,
the crossing gates and flashing lights,
the milk car, the pencil-size logs,

the metallic men and women,
the dangling water tower,
and the round mirror for a pond.

All I wanted was to be blinded
over and over by this shaking light
as the train stuck fast to its oval course.

Or better still, to close my eyes,
to stay there on the cold narrow rails
and let the train tunnel through me

the way it tunneled through the mountain
painted the color of rock,
and then there would be nothing

but the long whistling through the dark—
no basement, no boy,
no everlasting summer afternoon.

Building with Its Face Blown Off

How suddenly the private
is revealed in a bombed-out city,
how the blue and white striped wallpaper

of a second story bedroom is now
exposed to the lightly falling snow
as if the room had answered the explosion

wearing only its striped pajamas.
Some neighbors and soldiers
poke around in the rubble below

and stare up at the hanging staircase,
the portrait of a grandfather,
a door dangling from a single hinge.

And the bathroom looks almost embarrassed
by its uncovered ochre walls,
the twisted mess of its plumbing,

the sink sinking to its knees,
the ripped shower curtain,
the torn goldfish trailing bubbles.

It's like a dollhouse view
as if a child on its knees could reach in
and pick up the bureau, straighten a picture.

Or it might be a room on a stage
in a play with no characters,
no dialogue or audience,

no beginning, middle and end—
just the broken furniture in the street,
a shoe among the cinder blocks,

a light snow still falling
on a distant steeple, and people
crossing a bridge that still stands.

And beyond that—crows in a tree,
the statue of a leader on a horse,
and clouds that look like smoke,

and even farther on, in another country
on a blanket under a shade tree,
a man pouring wine into two glasses

and a woman sliding out
the wooden pegs of a wicker hamper
filled with bread, cheese, and several kinds of olives.

Special Glasses

I had to send away for them
because they are not available in any store.

They look the same as any sunglasses
with a light tint and silvery frames,
but instead of filtering out the harmful
rays of the sun,

they filter out the harmful sight of you—
you on the approach,
you waiting at my bus stop,
you, face in the evening window.

Every morning I put them on
and step out the side door
whistling a melody of thanks to my nose
and my ears for holding them in place, just so,

singing a song of gratitude
to the lens grinder at his heavy bench
and to the very lenses themselves
because they allow it all to come in, all but you.

How they know the difference
between the green hedges, the stone walls,
and you is beyond me,

yet the schoolbuses flashing in the rain
do come in, as well as the postman waving
and the mother and daughter dogs next door,

and then there is the tea kettle
about to play its chord—
everything sailing right in but you, girl.

Yes, just as the night air passes through the screen,
but not the mosquito,
and as water swirls down the drain,
but not the eggshell,
so the flowering trellis and the moon
pass through my special glasses, but not you.

Let us keep it this way, I say to myself,
as I lay my special glasses on the night table,
pull the chain on the lamp,
and say a prayer—unlike the song—
that I will not see you in my dreams.

THREE

The Lanyard

The other day as I was ricocheting slowly
off the pale blue walls of this room,
bouncing from typewriter to piano,
from bookshelf to an envelope lying on the floor,
I found myself in the L section of the dictionary
where my eyes fell upon the word *lanyard*.

No cookie nibbled by a French novelist
could send one more suddenly into the past—
a past where I sat at a workbench at a camp
by a deep Adirondack lake
learning how to braid thin plastic strips
into a lanyard, a gift for my mother.

I had never seen anyone use a lanyard
or wear one, if that's what you did with them,
but that did not keep me from crossing
strand over strand again and again
until I had made a boxy
red and white lanyard for my mother.

She gave me life and milk from her breasts,
and I gave her a lanyard.
She nursed me in many a sickroom,
lifted teaspoons of medicine to my lips,
set cold face-cloths on my forehead,
and then led me out into the airy light

and taught me to walk and swim,
and I, in turn, presented her with a lanyard.
Here are thousands of meals, she said,
and here is clothing and a good education.
And here is your lanyard, I replied,
which I made with a little help from a counselor.

Here is a breathing body and a beating heart,
strong legs, bones and teeth,
and two clear eyes to read the world, she whispered,
and here, I said, is the lanyard I made at camp.
And here, I wish to say to her now,
is a smaller gift—not the archaic truth

that you can never repay your mother,
but the rueful admission that when she took
the two-tone lanyard from my hands,
I was as sure as a boy could be
that this useless, worthless thing I wove
out of boredom would be enough to make us even.

Boy Shooting at a Statue

It was late afternoon,
the beginning of winter, a light snow,
and I was the only one in the small park

to witness the lone boy running
in circles around the base of a bronze statue.
I could not read the carved name

of the statesman who loomed above,
one hand on his cold hip,
but as the boy ran, head down,

he would point a finger at the statue
and pull an imaginary trigger
imitating the sounds of rapid gunfire.

Evening thickened, the mercury sank,
but the boy kept running in the circle
of his footprints in the snow

shooting blindly into the air.
History will never find a way to end,
I thought, as I left the park by the north gate

and walked slowly home
returning to the station of my desk
where the sheets of paper I wrote on

were like pieces of glass
through which I could see
hundreds of dark birds circling in the sky below.

Genius

was what they called you in high school
if you tripped on a shoelace in the hall
and all your books went flying.

Or if you walked into an open locker door,
you would be known as Einstein,
who imagined riding a streetcar into infinity.

Later, genius became someone
who could take a sliver of chalk and squire pi
a hundred places out beyond the decimal point,

or a man painting on his back on a scaffold,
or drawing a waterwheel in a margin,
or spinning out a little night music.

But earlier this week on a wooded path,
I thought the swans afloat on the reservoir
were the true geniuses,

the ones who had figured out how to fly,
how to be both beautiful and brutal,
and how to mate for life.

Twenty-four geniuses in all,
for I numbered them as Yeats had done,
deployed upon the calm, crystalline surface—

forty-eight if we count their white reflections,
or an even fifty if you want to throw in me
and the dog running up ahead,

who were at least smart enough to be out
that day—she sniffing the ground,
me with my head up in the bright morning air.

The Student

My poetry instruction book,
which I bought at an outdoor stall along the river,

contains many rules
about what to avoid and what to follow.

More than two people in a poem
is a crowd, is one.

Mention what clothes you are wearing
as you compose, is another.

Avoid the word *vortex*,
the word *velvety*, and the word *cicada*.

When at a loss for an ending,
have some brown hens standing in the rain.

Never admit that you revise.
And—always keep your poem in one season.

I try to be mindful,
but in these last days of summer

whenever I look up from my page
and see a burn-mark of yellow leaves,

I think of the icy winds
that will soon be knifing through my jacket.

Reaper

As I drove north along a country road
on a bright spring morning
I caught the look of a man on the roadside
who was carrying an enormous scythe on his shoulder.

He was not wearing a long black cloak
with a hood to conceal his skull—
rather a torn white tee-shirt
and a pair of loose khaki trousers.

But still, as I flew past him,
he turned and met my glance
as if I had an appointment in Samarra,
not just the usual lunch at the Raccoon Lodge.

There was no sign I could give him
in that instant—no casual wave,
or thumbs-up, no two-fingered V
that would ease the jolt of fear

whose voltage ran from my ankles
to my scalp—just the glimpse,
the split-second lock of the pupils
like catching the eye of a stranger on a passing train.

And there was nothing to do
but keep driving, turn off the radio,
and notice how white the houses were,
how red the barns, and green the sloping fields.

The Order of the Day

A morning after a week of rain
and the sun shot down through the branches
into the tall, bare windows.

The brindled cat rolled over on his back,
and I could hear you in the kitchen
grinding coffee beans into a powder.

Everything seemed especially vivid
because I knew we were all going to die,
first the cat, then you, then me,

then somewhat later the liquefied sun
was the order I was envisioning.
But then again, you never really know.

The cat had a fiercely healthy look,
his coat so bristling and electric
I wondered what you had been feeding him

and what you had been feeding me
as I turned a corner
and beheld you out there on the sunny deck

lost in exercise, running in place,
knees lifted high, skin glistening—
and that toothy, immortal-looking smile of yours.

Constellations

Yes, that's Orion over there,
the three studs of the belt
clearly lined up just off the horizon.

And if you turn around you can see
Gemini, very visible tonight,
the twins looking off into space as usual.

That cluster a little higher in the sky
is Cassiopeia sitting in her astral chair
if I'm not mistaken.

And directly overhead,
isn't that Virginia Woolf
slipping along the River Ouse

in her inflatable canoe?
See the wide-brimmed hat and there,
the outline of the paddle, raised and dripping stars?

The Drive

There were four of us in the car
early that summer evening,
short-hopping from one place to another,
thrown together by a light toss of circumstance.

I was in the backseat
directly behind the driver who was talking
about one thing and another
while his wife smiled quietly at the windshield.

I was happy to be paying attention
to the rows of tall hedges
and the gravel driveways we were passing
and then the yellow signs on the roadside stores.

It was only when he began to belittle you
that I found myself shifting my focus
to the back of his head,
a head that was large and expansively bald.

As he continued talking
and the car continued along the highway,
I began to divide his head into sections
by means of dotted lines,

the kind you see on the diagram of a steer.
Only here, I was not interested in short loin,

rump, shank, or sirloin tip,
but curious about what region of his cranium

housed the hard nugget of his malice.
Tom, my friend, you would have enjoyed the sight—
the car turning this way and that,
the sunlight low in the trees,

the man going on about your many failings,
and me sitting quietly behind him
wearing my white butcher's apron
and my small, regulation butcher's hat.

On Not Finding You at Home

Usually you appear at the front door
when you hear my steps on the gravel,
but today the door was closed,
not a wisp of pale smoke from the chimney.

I peered into a window
but there was nothing but a table with a comb,
some yellow flowers in a glass of water
and dark shadows in the corners of the room.

I stood for a while under the big tree
and listened to the wind and the birds,
your wind and your birds,
your dark green woods beyond the clearing.

This is not what it is like to be you,
I realized as a few of your magnificent clouds
flew over the rooftop.
It is just me thinking about being you.

And before I headed back down the hill,
I walked in a circle around your house,
making an invisible line
which you would have to cross before dark.

The Centrifuge

It is difficult to describe what we felt
after we paid the admission,
entered the aluminum dome,

and stood there with our mouths open
before the machine itself,
what we had only read about in the papers.

Huge and glistening it was
but bolted down and giving nothing away.

What did it mean?
we all openly wondered,
and did another machine exist somewhere else—
an even mightier one—
that was designed to be its exact opposite?

These were not new questions,
but we asked them earnestly and repeatedly.

Later, when we were home again—
a family of six having tea—
we raised these questions once more,
knowing that this made us part
of a great historical discussion
that included science
as well as literature and the weather

not to mention the lodger downstairs,
who, someone said,
had been seen earlier leaving the house
with a suitcase and a tightly furled umbrella.

The Introduction

I don't think this next poem
needs any introduction—
it's best to let the work speak for itself.

Maybe I should just mention
that whenever I use the word *five*,
I'm referring to that group of Russian composers
who came to be known as "The Five,"
Balakirev, Moussorgsky, Borodin—that crowd.

Oh—and Hypsicles was a Greek astronomer.
He did something with the circle.

That's about it, but for the record,
"Grimké" is Angelina Emily Grimké, the abolitionist.
"Imroz" is that little island near the Dardanelles.
"Monad"—well, you all know what a monad is.

There could be a little problem
with *mastaba*, which is one of those Egyptian
above-ground sepulchers, sort of brick and limestone.

And you're all familiar with helminthology?
It's the science of worms.

Oh, and you will recall that Phoebe Mozee
is the real name of Annie Oakley.

Other than that, everything should be obvious.
Wagga Wagga is in New South Wales.
Rhyolite is that soft volcanic rock.
What else?
Yes, *meranti* is a type of timber, in tropical Asia I think,
and Rahway is just Rahway, New Jersey.

The rest of the poem should be clear.
I'll just read it and let it speak for itself.

It's about the time I went picking wild strawberries.

It's called "Picking Wild Strawberries."

FOUR

The Revenant

I am the dog you put to sleep,
as you like to call the needle of oblivion,
come back to tell you this simple thing:
I never liked you—not one bit.

When I licked your face,
I thought of biting off your nose.
When I watched you toweling yourself dry,
I wanted to leap and unman you with a snap.

I resented the way you moved,
your lack of animal grace,
the way you would sit in a chair to eat,
a napkin on your lap, knife in your hand.

I would have run away,
but I was too weak, a trick you taught me
while I was learning to sit and heel,
and—greatest of insults—shake hands without a hand.

I admit the sight of the leash
would excite me
but only because it meant I was about
to smell things you had never touched.

You do not want to believe this,
but I have no reason to lie.

I hated the car, the rubber toys,
disliked your friends and, worse, your relatives.

The jingling of my tags drove me mad.
You always scratched me in the wrong place.
All I ever wanted from you
was food and fresh water in my metal bowls.

While you slept, I watched you breathe
as the moon rose in the sky.
It took all of my strength
not to raise my head and howl.

Now I am free of the collar,
the yellow raincoat, monogrammed sweater,
the absurdity of your lawn,
and that is all you need to know about this place

except what you already supposed
and are glad it did not happen sooner—
that everyone here can read and write,
the dogs in poetry, the cats and all the others in prose.

See No Evil

No one expected all three of them
to sit there on their tree stumps forever,
their senses covered with their sinuous paws
so as to shut out the vile, nefarious world.

As it happened,
it was the one on the left
who was the first to desert his post,
uncupping his ears,
then loping off into the orbit of rumors and lies,
but also into the realm of symphonies,
the sound of water tumbling over rocks
and wind stirring the leafy domes of trees.

Then the monkey on the right lowered his hands
from his wide mouth and slipped away
in search of someone to talk to,
some news he could spread,
maybe something to curse or shout about.

And that left the monkey in the middle
alone with his silent vigil,
shielding his eyes from depravity's spectacle,
blind to the man whipping his horse,
the woman shaking her baby in the air,
but also unable to see

the russet sun on a rough shelf of rock
and apples in the grass at the base of a tree.

Sometimes, he wonders about the other two,
listens for the faint sounds of their breathing
up there on the mantel
alongside the clock and the candlesticks.

And some nights in the quiet house
he wishes he could break the silence with a question,

but he knows the one on his right
would not be able to hear,
and the one to his left,
according to their sacred oath—
the one they all took with one paw raised—
is forbidden forever to speak, even in reply.

Freud

I think I know what he would say
about the dream I had last night
in which my nose was lopped off in a sword fight,
leaving me to wander the streets of 18th-century Paris
with a kind of hideous blowhole in the middle of my face.

But what would be his thoughts
about the small brown leather cone
attached to my face with goose grease
which I purchased from a gnome-like sales clerk
at a little shop called House of a Thousand Noses?

And how would he interpret
my stopping before every gilded mirror
to admire the fine grain and the tiny brass studs,
always turning to show my best profile,
my clean-shaven chin slightly raised?

Surely, narcissism fails to capture
my love of posing in those many rooms,
sometimes with an open window behind me
showing the blue sky which would be eclipsed
by the Eiffel Tower in roughly a hundred years.

Height

Viewed from the roof of a tall building,
people on the street
are said to take on the appearance of ants,

but I have been up here for so long,
gazing down over this parapet,
that the ants below have begun to resemble people.

Look at that one lingering
near a breadcrumb on the curb,
does he not share the appearance of my brother-in-law?

And the beautiful young ant
in the light summer dress
with the smooth, ovoid head,

the one heading up the lamppost—
could she not double for my favorite cousin
with her glad eyes and her pulled-back hair?

Surely, one with the face
of my mother and another with the posture
of my father will soon go hobbling by.

The Lodger

After I had beaten my sword into a ploughshare,
I beat my ploughshare into a hoe,
then beat the hoe into a fork,
which I used to eat my dinner alone.

And when I had finished dinner,
I beat my fork into a toothpick,
which I twirled on my lips
then flicked over a low stone wall

as I walked along the city river
under the clouds and stars,
quite happy but for the thought
that I should have beaten that toothpick into a shilling

so I could buy a newspaper to read
after climbing the stairs to my room.

Class Picture, 1954

I am the third one
from the left in the third row.

The girl I have been in love with
since the 5th grade is just behind me
to the right, the one with the bangs.

The boy who pushes me down
in the playground
is the last one on the left in the top row.

And my friend Paul is the second one
in the second row, the one
with his collar sticking out, next to the teacher.

But that's not all—
if you look carefully you can see
our house in the background

with its porch and its brick chimney
and up in the clouds
you can see the faces of my parents,

and over there, off to the side,
Superman is balancing
a green car over his head with one hand.

Care and Feeding

Because tomorrow
I will turn 420 in dog years,
I have decided to take myself
for a long walk on the path around the lake,

and when I get back to the house,
I will jump up on my chest
and lick my nose, my ears and eyelids
while I tell myself again and again to get down.

Then I will replenish my bowl
with cold water from the tap
and hand myself a biscuit from the jar
which I will hold gingerly in my teeth.

Then I will make three circles
and lie down on the wood floor at my feet
and close my eyes
as I type all morning and into the afternoon,

checking every once in a while
to make sure I am still there,
reaching down with one hand
to stroke my furry, esteemed, venerable head.

Carry

I want to carry you
and for you to carry me
the way voices are said to carry over water.

Just this morning on the shore,
I could hear two people talking quietly
in a rowboat on the far side of the lake.

They were talking about fishing,
then one changed the subject,
and, I swear, they began talking about you.

Drawing Class

If you ever asked me
how my drawing classes are going,

I would tell you that I enjoy
adhering to the outline of a thing,

to follow the slope of an individual pear
or the curve of a glossy piano.

And I love trailing my hand
over the smooth membrane of bond,

the intelligent little trinity
of my fingers gripping the neck of the pencil

while the other two dangle below
like the fleshy legs of a tiny swimmer.

I would add that I can get lost
crosshatching the shadow of a chair

or tracing and retracing
the slight undercarriage of a breast.

Even the preparations call out to me—
taping the paper to a wooden board,

brushing its surface clean,
and sharpening a few pencils to a fine point.

The thin hexagonal pencil
is mightier than the pen,

for it can modulate from firm to faint
and shift from thin to broad

whenever it leans more acutely over the page—
the bright yellow pencil,

which is also mightier than the sword
for there is no erasing what the sword can do.

We all started with the box and the ball
then moved on to the cup and the lamp,

the serrated leaf, the acorn with its cap.
But I want to graduate to the glass decanter

and learn how to immobilize in lead
translucent curtains lifted in the air.

I want to draw
four straight lines that will connect me

to the four points of the compass,
to the bright spires of cities,

the overlapping trellises,
the turning spokes of the world.

One day I want to draw freehand
a continuous figure

that will begin with me
when the black tip touches the paper

and end with you when it is lifted
and set down beside a luminous morning window.

The Flying Notebook

With its spiraling metal body
and white pages for wings,
my notebook flies over my bed while I sleep—

a bird full of quotations and tiny images
who loves the night's dark rooms,
glad now to be free of my scrutiny and my pen point.

Tomorrow, it will go with me
into the streets where I may stop to look
at my reflection in a store window,

and later I may break a piece of bread
at a corner table in a restaurant
then scribble something down.

But tonight it flies around me in circles
sailing through a column of moonlight,
then beating its paper wings even more,

once swooping so low
as to ripple the surface of a lake
in a dream in which I happen to be drowning.

Fool Me Good

I am under the covers
waiting for the heat to come up
with a gurgle and hiss
and the banging of the water hammer
that will frighten the cold out of the room.

And I am listening to a blues singer
named Precious Bryant
singing a song called "Fool Me Good."

If you don't love me, baby, she sings,
would you please try to fool me good?

I am also stroking the dog's head
and writing down these words,
which means that I am calmly flying
in the face of the Buddhist advice
to do only one thing at a time.

Just pour the tea,
just look into the eye of the flower,
just sing the song—
one thing at a time

and you will achieve serenity,
which is what I would love to do
as the fan-blades of the morning begin to turn.

If you don't love me, baby,
she sings
as a day-moon fades in the window
and the hands circle the clock,
would you please try to fool me good?

Yes, Precious, I reply,
I will fool you as good as I can,
but first I have to learn to listen to you
with my whole heart,
and not until you have finished

will I put on my slippers,
squeeze out some toothpaste,
and make a big foamy face in the mirror,

freshly dedicated to doing one thing at a time—
one note at a time for you, darling,
one tooth at a time for me.

Evening Alone

Last of the strong sun
on white tiles, stack of white towels,
faint piano melody from downstairs,
and the downpour of hot water on my shoulders.

I lift my face to the nozzle, close my eyes
and see mountains folded
over mountains,
smoke rising from a woodcutter's hut,
and in the distance, billowing pastel clouds.

It must be China I am beholding
on this early summer evening—
the great sway of rivers,
thousands of birds rising on the wing,
the jade and mulberries of China,
plum blossoms—now the cry of a pheasant.

It is a vision that drains me of desire,
and leaves me wanting nothing
but to be here
in this hot steamy room
washing my neck, rubbing my sides,

the soap slithering down the chest and stomach,
eyes still shut as I picture in China
a light boat crossing a lake

and a wooden house on the shore
where a young woman in a tight-fitting silk dress
lifts a cup of cinnamon tea
to her painted, slightly parted lips.

The Trouble with Poetry

The trouble with poetry, I realized
as I walked along a beach one night—
cold Florida sand under my bare feet,
a show of stars in the sky—

the trouble with poetry is
that it encourages the writing of more poetry,
more guppies crowding the fish tank,
more baby rabbits
hopping out of their mothers into the dewy grass.

And how will it ever end?
unless the day finally arrives
when we have compared everything in the world
to everything else in the world,

and there is nothing left to do
but quietly close our notebooks
and sit with our hands folded on our desks.

Poetry fills me with joy
and I rise like a feather in the wind.
Poetry fills me with sorrow
and I sink like a chain flung from a bridge.

But mostly poetry fills me
with the urge to write poetry,

to sit in the dark and wait for a little flame
to appear at the tip of my pencil.

And along with that, the longing to steal,
to break into the poems of others
with a flashlight and a ski mask.

And what an unmerry band of thieves we are,
cut-purses, common shoplifters,
I thought to myself
as a cold wave swirled around my feet
and the lighthouse moved its megaphone over the sea,
which is an image I stole directly
from Lawrence Ferlinghetti—
to be perfectly honest for a moment—

the bicycling poet of San Francisco
whose little amusement park of a book
I carried in a side pocket of my uniform
up and down the treacherous halls of high school.

Silence

There is the sudden silence of the crowd
above a motionless player on the field,
and the silence of the orchid.

The silence of the falling vase
before it strikes the floor,
the silence of the belt when it is not striking the child.

The stillness of the cup and the water in it,
the silence of the moon
and the quiet of the day far from the roar of the sun.

The silence when I hold you to my chest,
the silence of the window above us,
and the silence when you rise and turn away.

And there is the silence of this morning
which I have broken with my pen,
a silence that had piled up all night

like snow falling in the darkness of the house—
the silence before I wrote a word
and the poorer silence now.

Acknowledgments

Grateful acknowledgment is made to the editors of the following periodicals, where these poems first appeared, some in slightly different versions:

The American Scholar: "Boy Shooting at a Statue"
Atlanta Review: "Bereft," "The Drive," "The Introduction"
The Atlantic Monthly: "The Peasants' Revolt"
Bat City Review: "The Student"
Boulevard: "Breathless," "Eastern Standard Time," "The Flying Notebook"
The Cortland Review: "I Ask You"
Field: "Silence," "You, Reader"
Five Points: "Care and Feeding," "Carry," "The Lanyard," "The Order of the Day," "The Revenant"
Fulcrum: "The Centrifuge"
The Gettysburg Review: "Special Glasses," "Theme"
Hotel Amerika: "Evening Alone," "Monday"
Living Forge: "See No Evil"
London Review of Books: "Building with Its Face Blown Off"

The Massachusetts Review: "Flock"

Michigan Quarterly Review: "Constellations"

Mississippi Review: "Drawing Class"

New Delta Review: "In the Evening"

The New Yorker: "Statues in the Park"

Nightsun: "The Trouble with Poetry"

Oxford American: "Fool Me Good"

The Paris Review: "Freud"

Poetry: "Boyhood," "Genius," "The Long Day," "In the Moment,"
    "Silence," "Traveling Alone"

Van Gogh's Ear: "Height"

Washington Square Review: "Class Picture, 1954"

Western Humanities Review: "On Not Finding You at Home"

"The Centrifuge" was selected by Lyn Hejinian for *The Best American Poetry: 2004*, series ed. David Lehman (New York: Scribners, 2004).

Thanks also to Gina Centrello, Dan Menaker, Julia Cheiffetz, and Jynne Martin of Random House, for their support and guidance; to Chris Calhoun, for his friendship and exuberant representation; and to Diane, my true in-house editor.

BILLY COLLINS is the author of nine collections of poetry, including *Nine Horses; Sailing Alone Around the Room; Picnic, Lightning; The Art of Drowning;* and *Questions About Angels.* He is also the editor of *Poetry 180: A Turning Back to Poetry* and *180 More: Extraordinary Poems for Every Day.* A Distinguished Professor of English at Lehman College of the City University of New York, he was appointed Poet Laureate of the United States from 2001 to 2003 and is currently serving as the Poet Laureate of New York State.

ABOUT THE TYPE

The text of this book was set in Filosofia. It was designed in 1996 by Zuzana Licko, who created it for digital typesetting as an interpretation of the sixteenth-century typeface Bodoni. Filosofia, an example of Licko's unusual font designs, has classical proportions with a strong feeling, softened by rounded droplike serifs. She has designed many typefaces and is the cofounder of *Emigre* magazine, where many of them first appeared. Born in Bratislava, Czechoslovakia, Licko came to the United States in 1968. She studied graphic communications at the University of California at Berkeley, graduating in 1984.